INTRODUCTION

The pleasures of handwork in general and quilting in particular have long been acknowledged, but it is only recently that leisure time and the machine age have permitted quilting to go from the creating of necessities to the creating of luxuries. No longer do we need quilts just for bedding, and we can, therefore, indulge in the making of quilted pieces for the sheer joy of working in the media. Many of us, however, simply do not have the time or the inclination to make an entire quilt, or we don't want to undertake the making of a quilt as a first project. In answer to the numerous questions of "what to quilt if not a quilt," I have written *Patchwork Pillows*.

This book contains full-size templates and instructions for making twelve patchwork pillows. The pillow designs are all based upon actual quilt blocks. Once you have mastered the technique of working with patchwork by making a pillow, you may want to use the templates to make a full-size quilt by making and joining additional quilt blocks.

Since the pillows are not all the same size, I have given the size of the finished pillow at the beginning of each design. I have also indicated fabric requirements for the pieces and for the backing fabric. Since the back of the pillow is exposed, coordinate the color of the backing fabric to the color scheme of the pillow. The simplest way to do this is to choose for the backing fabric one of the fabrics used for the pieces. In addition to the special materials listed for the individual pillows, each pillow will require thin, unbleached muslin or other cotton fabric for a lining, polyester quilting fabric and material for stuffing the finished pillow—either polyester fiber filling or a pillow form.

Before beginning to work on your pillow, read through the general instructions for mak-

ing a patchwork pillow. These general instructions are not repeated with each pillow. However, many times simple hints can help prevent hours of frustration, and so deviations from the general instructions are noted with the individual pillows.

The color schemes specified are only meant as guidelines. Feel free to use your own color choices. I like to draw some small facsimiles of the designs and, using colored pencils, color in the shapes, alternating the colors to get an idea of how the finished piece will look. You will find that the colors are not always interchangeable with the pieces. For instance, *Pieced Star* looks altogether different if the "red" pieces are done in a light blue print, instead of vice versa. You have to decide what combination is the most pleasing to you. I feel it is also important to balance patterned pieces with solids.

As for fabrics, I prefer to combine like fabrics—cotton with linen, silk with satin and/or velvet. But again, let your judgment guide you. If you like the way it looks, that's all that matters. If possible use fabrics that will not easily fray when cut. The pillows in this book have all been done in cotton or cotton blends. A batiste was used on the *Double Monkey Wrench* pillow, but it was lined with a heavier cotton. On the *Bow Tie* pillow and the *Double Monkey Wrench* pillow, chintz was also used. If this is your first attempt at piecing and quilting, chintz is not highly recommended. There is virtually no "give" to it and it requires more patience to get the pieces to fit precisely. I also find it best not to quilt through chintz pieces, but rather around them.

TEMPLATES

All of the pattern pieces used in making these pillows are given in actual-size templates printed on special heavyweight paper in the center of this book. Locate the designated template and carefully cut it out. It is important that the templates be cut out carefully because, if they are not accurate, the fabric pieces will not fit together. Use a pair of good-size sharp scissors, a single-edged razor blade or an X-acto knife. Be careful not to bend the fine corners of the triangles.

WHERE TO START

Before starting the square, make sure that all the fabric is pressed smoothly to eliminate any wrinkles. Have all of the supplies ready: appropriate templates, scissors, ruler and sharp pencil. For marking dark fabrics, I use a chalk pencil, available in most fabric stores. It comes in a variety of pale colors, including white, and is thus much easier to see on dark fabrics.

It is important to keep the fabric on a hard surface to get a good clean line while tracing the template, but I have often found it extremely difficult to keep the fabric from slipping and moving under the template. A piece of felt, placed on the table or desk top under the fabric, will prevent the fabric from slipping, but will not make the surface so soft as to cause the pencil to break through the fabric.

CUTTING THE PIECES

Cutting is one of the most important steps in making any kind of patchwork. You must be accurate in order to have the pattern fit perfectly. Take one of the templates and refer to the instructions to find out how many pieces of each fabric you need to complete the pillow. You may want to jot this information down in pencil on the pattern piece itself, i.e., 4 G(reen), 8 W(hite), etc.

These templates are the exact size the patch will be after sewing is done, and they have purposely been printed *without* the ¼" seam allowance. Lay the cardboard template on the wrong side of the fabric, being careful to see that the longest part of the pattern piece runs parallel to the straight of the grain. Trace around the cardboard with a hard lead pencil or chalk. Now measure ¼" around the shape. Using a ruler, draw this second line. This is the line you will cut on. Now you will see that the first line (where you traced the template) is there to use as a guide for stitching. If the

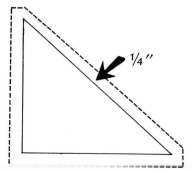

Broken line is the cutting line. Solid line is the seam line; match to the line on the next patch. Sewing is done on this solid line.

seam allowance is not perfect, this will not show; but the *sewing line* must be perfectly straight and true, or the patches will not come together into a perfectly shaped design. As each piece is traced, add the ¼" around it before going on to the next piece. I find it easier to have the pieces share a common cutting line, but if this is confusing, leave a narrow border or margin around each piece.

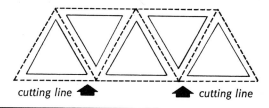

cutting line ◄━━   ━━► *cutting line*

Cut out the required number of pieces from each fabric and put them all together in a plastic bag large enough to hold them without creasing. If you are making the *Pine Tree* pillow, you may find that Piece No. 4 will be too large to fit into your bag, so just keep this piece aside.

SEWING

There are two ways to sew the pieces together—either by hand or by machine. I know that the purists say "always by hand," but my feeling is that you should do what you prefer. Let time and occasion dictate the process. Obviously, driving across country doesn't lend itself to piecing by machine. But, if you decide on Thursday that you want that new pillow on the couch for weekend guests to see, it doesn't make much sense to do it all by hand. I very often piece by machine and quilt by hand. If you are planning to piece by hand use the back stitch. Whether you piece by machine or by hand, remember to stitch on

PATCHWORK PILLOWS
with Step-by-Step Instructions
and Full-Size Templates

JUDY LEVY

Dover Publications, Inc., New York

Published in Canada by General Publishing Company, Ltd., 30 Lesmill Road, Don Mills, Toronto, Ontario.
Published in the United Kingdom by Constable and Company, Ltd., 10 Orange Street, London WC2H 7EG.

Patchwork Pillows with Step-by-Step Instructions and Full-Size Templates is a new work, first published by Dover Publications, Inc. in 1977.

International Standard Book Number: 0-486-23473-8
Library of Congress Catalog Card Number: 76-47804

Manufactured in the United States of America
Dover Publications, Inc.
180 Varick Street
New York, N. Y. 10014

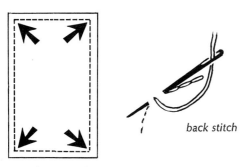

Keep margins open at corners.

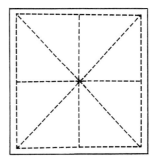

back stitch

the sewing line, being very careful not to stitch into the margins at corners. Once the pieces are sewn together, press everything flat, keeping the seams closed and going in one direction.

QUILTING

Sometimes the quilting design becomes a part of the pillow design, as in the *White House Steps* pillow. Other times it is used to accent a part of the patchwork, as in the *Combination Star* pillow where the quilting is done within the seams, so that it only puffs the existing design. If the quilting is done within the seamlines, the seams themselves will serve as guidelines, and no other markings need be made on the block. If the quilting pattern is to show as decoration on top of the deisgn as in the *Wedding Ring* pillow, guidelines must be drawn on the patchwork to help keep the stitches straight. These guidelines are traced on the pillow top after the patchwork is completed and before the quilting fiber is basted. I have found the chalk pencil mentioned earlier a very satisfactory medium. The colors are light and will wear off, leaving only your stitches showing. Regular lead pencil can also be used, but it will not wear off as readily as the chalk. The *White House Steps* pillow is quilted with hearts, and I have given templates for these designs in the template section. Remember that templates for patchwork are traced on the *wrong* side and templates or designs for quilting are traced on the *right* side.

There are many varieties of quilting fiber available on the market. For pillows I prefer a fairly thin polyester quilting fiber. It comes in large sheets, usually packaged according to bed size. Cut a piece about ½" larger all around

than the finished patchwork. Do the same with a piece of thin, unbleached muslin or other cotton fabric that will be the lining for your patchwork. The three layers are now put together like a sandwich: first the patchwork piece, then the quilting fabric and last the lining. Pin all three layers together and then fasten them securely with large basting stitches. Start in the center of the block, and sew toward the edges until you have a number of intersecting lines.

Starting in the center, fasten the layers securely with a number of intersecting lines.

Now to quilt! *Always work from the center out.* Otherwise you are apt to end up with a large lump in the middle. The actual quilt stitching is a simple process for any one who can sew. A simple running stitch is used, but it does take a little practice. The stitch should be fairly small and close together. This is the reason for choosing a thin quilting fiber; a thicker fiber would make the quilting more difficult.

running stitch

After using a variety of needles, I recommend the short, fine quilting needle. It allows a rhythm to develop fairly quickly so that the quilting is even and smooth. It is much more difficult to do the running stitch with any speed using a longer needle. But again, use what works best for you. I prefer using No. 50 cotton thread. To begin, make a knot at the end of the thread and bring the needle through to the top of the patchwork, then pull gently but firmly and the knot will slip through the lower layer into the padding, where it will not be seen. To finish off, make a single back stitch and run the thread through the padding. Cut, and the end will be lost. I do not use a frame or hoop when I work on a pillow, but this is a matter of personal preference.

FINISHING THE PILLOW

1. Measure your quilted top and cut a piece of backing fabric the size of the quilted piece.

2. Right sides together, pin around 3½ sides, leaving a large enough opening at one side to allow you to turn the whole piece right side out after stitching.

Sew around 3½ sides. Round the corners slightly.

3. Now stitch around the outside where you have pinned, being careful not to let the design get stitched into the seam allowance. As you stitch around the corners, round them slightly, even though the design is square. This will prevent very pointed corners that are difficult to turn and impossible to stuff.

4. Turn right side out and check the stitching, making certain that none of the pattern is caught in the seam allowance and that there is no puckering. Once you have determined that the pillow is to your liking, turn it once more to the wrong side and trim the margins so that they are no more than ¼". Be careful not to clip the stitches.

5. Turn the pillow right side out again and begin to stuff. I use a polyester fiber filling recommended by the manufacturer for stuffing pillows and toys. Work the fiber into the corners.

6. When you have stuffed the pillow to the

desired fullness, turn in the open edge and blind stitch.

7. If you prefer, you can use a pillow form. These forms are available in even sizes only (12", 14", 16", etc.) If you use a form, you will probably want to leave one whole side open to facilitate stuffing.

8. If you are planning to use a ruffle or other edging, baste it in place on the right side of the pillow after step 1. Then proceed from step 2 to make the completed pillow. Pre-ruffled trimming uses only as much yardage as the measurement of all four sides of the pillow plus an additional 2" for overlap where the ends meet. For instance, if the pillow is a

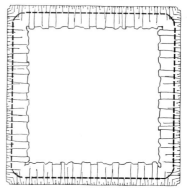

Baste edging material in place on right side of pillow.

15" square, you will need about 62" of pre-ruffled trimming (15" x 4, plus 2"). If the ruffling material is not pre-ruffled, you will need double the length of each side plus the extra 2" for overlap. A 15"-square pillow will need 122" of the unruffled edging material.

METRIC CONVERSION TABLE

¼"=6mm	¼ yard=23cm
½"=13mm	1/3 yard=30cm
1"=25mm	½ yard=46cm
14"=36cm	⅝ yard=58cm
15"=38cm	2/3 yard=62cm
17"=43cm	1 yard=92cm

PATCHWORK
PILLOWS

PIECED STAR PILLOW

SIZE OF FINISHED PILLOW: 15″ SQUARE

MATERIALS

¼ yard of each color fabric for piecing.
½ yard fabric for backing.

LEGEND

(W) White
(B) Blue
(R) Red
(WP) White Print
(BP) Blue Print

NUMBER OF PIECES TO BE CUT

Piece No. 1 . . . . .4 White
Piece No. 2 . . . . .4 White Print
Piece No. 3 . . . . .8 Blue
Piece No. 3 . . . . .4 Blue Print
Piece No. 3 . . . . .4 Red

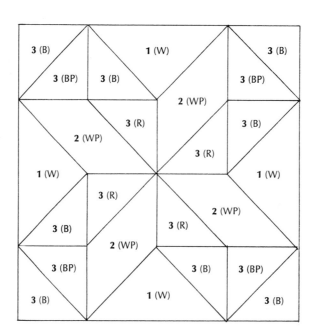

Templates for this pillow appear on Plate A.

PIECED STAR PILLOW

This pillow was pieced and quilted by machine.

JACK-IN-THE-BOX PILLOW

SIZE OF FINISHED PILLOW: 15″ SQUARE

MATERIALS

¼ yard of each color fabric for piecing.
½ yard fabric for backing.

LEGEND

(Y) Yellow
(B) Black
(WP) Blue Print
(BP) Black Print

NUMBER OF PIECES TO BE CUT

Piece No. 1 . . . . .4 Black
Piece No. 2 . . . . .4 Black Print
Piece No. 3 . . . . .16 Yellow
Piece No. 4 . . . . .1 Black
Piece No. 5 . . . . .4 Blue Print

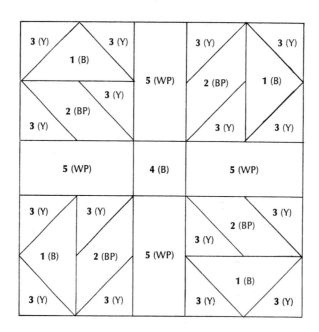

Templates for this pillow appear on Plate B.

4

JACK-IN-THE-BOX PILLOW

This pillow was pieced by machine and quilted by hand around the large triangular shapes formed by template 1 and the center square formed by template 4.

WEDDING RING PILLOW

SIZE OF FINISHED PILLOW: 14" SQUARE

MATERIALS

¼ yard of each color fabric for piecing.
½ yard fabric for backing.

LEGEND

(Y) Yellow
(BP) Brown Print
(G) Green
(O) Orange

NUMBER OF PIECES TO BE CUT

Piece No. 1 ....4 Brown Print
Piece No. 1 ....8 Yellow
Piece No. 1 ....8 Orange
Piece No. 2 ....5 Brown Print
Piece No. 2 ....4 Orange
Piece No. 3 ....4 Green

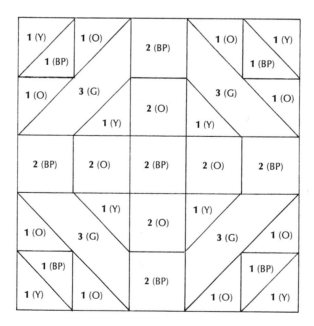

Templates for this pillow appear on Plate C.

6

WEDDING RING PILLOW

This pillow was pieced and quilted by hand. It is filled with a ready-made pillow form.

WHITE HOUSE STEPS PILLOW

SIZE OF FINISHED PILLOW: 15″ WITHOUT RUFFLE

MATERIALS

¼ yard of each color fabric for piecing.
½ yard fabric for backing.
The ruffle in the sample pillow was made with 4 yards of lace that was not pre-ruffled.

LEGEND

(R) Raspberry
(S) Stripes
(RP) Raspberry Print I
(WP) Raspberry Print II

NUMBER OF PIECES TO BE CUT

Piece No. 1 ....4 Raspberry
Piece No. 2 ....2 Stripes
Piece No. 3 ....1 Raspberry Print II
Piece No. 4 ....2 Stripes
Piece No. 4 ....4 Raspberry Print I

1 (R)	4 (RP)	1 (R)
4 (RP)	4 (S)	4 (RP)
	2 (S) 3 (WP) 2 (S)	
	4 (S)	
1 (R)	4 (RP)	1 (R)

Templates for this pillow appear on Plates D and E.

8

WHITE HOUSE STEPS PILLOW

This pillow was pieced by machine and quilted by hand in heart shapes. Templates for the quilting shapes are given in the template section. Follow the instructions in the introduction for transferring these shapes to the pillow. The largest heart is used in the center; the medium-sized heart in the outer border and the small heart in the inner border. See page vi for instructions on adding the ruffle.

COMBINATION STAR PILLOW

SIZE OF FINISHED PILLOW: 17″ SQUARE

MATERIALS

¼ yard of each color fabric for piecing.
⅝ yard fabric for backing.

LEGEND

(G) Green
(RG) Red Gingham
(B) Blue
(R) Red
(Y) Yellow Print
(BP) Black Print

NUMBER OF PIECES TO BE CUT

Piece No. 1 . . . . .16 Green
Piece No. 1 . . . . .4 Red
Piece No. 2 . . . . .1 Yellow Print
Piece No. 2 . . . . .4 Black Print
Piece No. 3 . . . . .8 Blue
Piece No. 3 . . . . .8 Red Gingham

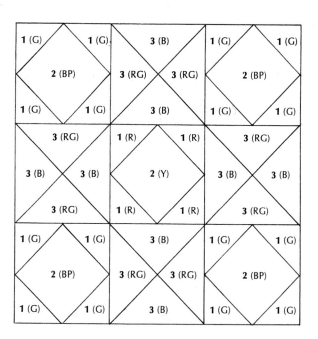

Templates for this pillow appear on Plate F.

Combination Star Pillow continues after templates.

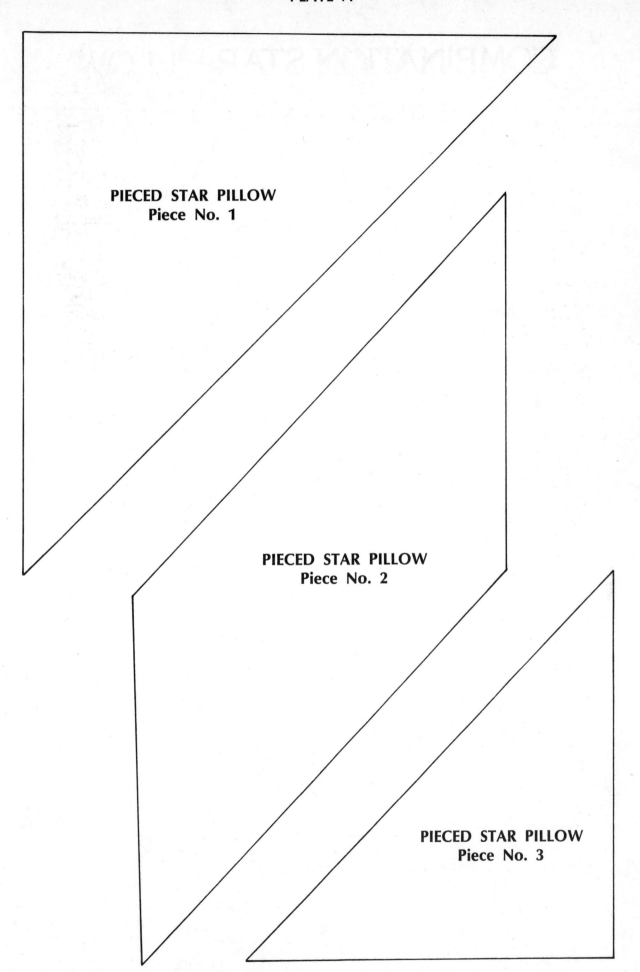

PIECED STAR PILLOW
Piece No. 1

PIECED STAR PILLOW
Piece No. 2

PIECED STAR PILLOW
Piece No. 3

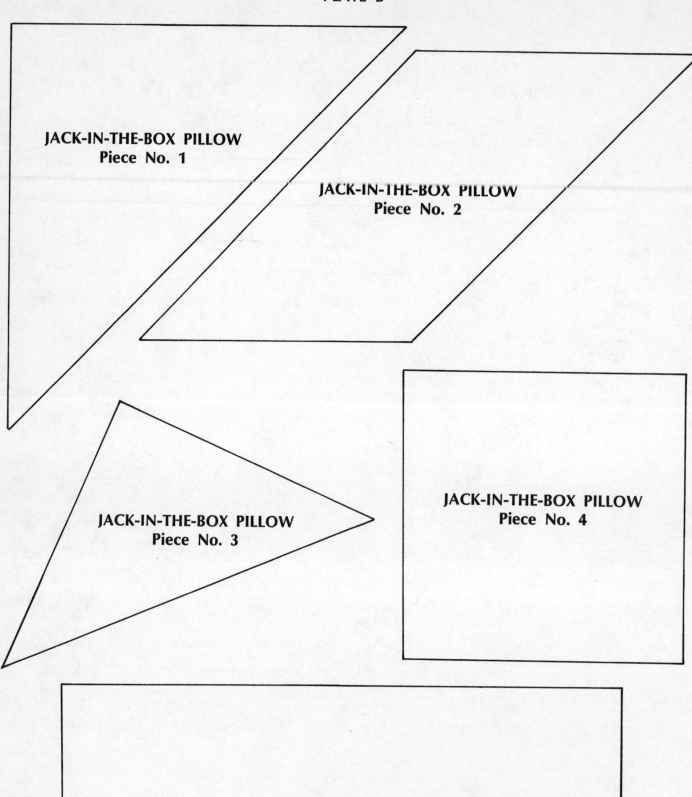

JACK-IN-THE-BOX PILLOW
Piece No. 1

JACK-IN-THE-BOX PILLOW
Piece No. 2

JACK-IN-THE-BOX PILLOW
Piece No. 3

JACK-IN-THE-BOX PILLOW
Piece No. 4

JACK-IN-THE-BOX PILLOW
Piece No. 5

PLATE C

WEDDING RING PILLOW
Piece No. 1

WEDDING RING PILLOW
Piece No. 2

**WEDDING RING
PILLOW**
Piece No. 3

WHITE HOUSE STEPS PILLOW
Piece No. 1

WHITE HOUSE STEPS PILLOW
Piece No. 2

WHITE HOUSE STEPS PILLOW
Piece No. 4

PLATE E

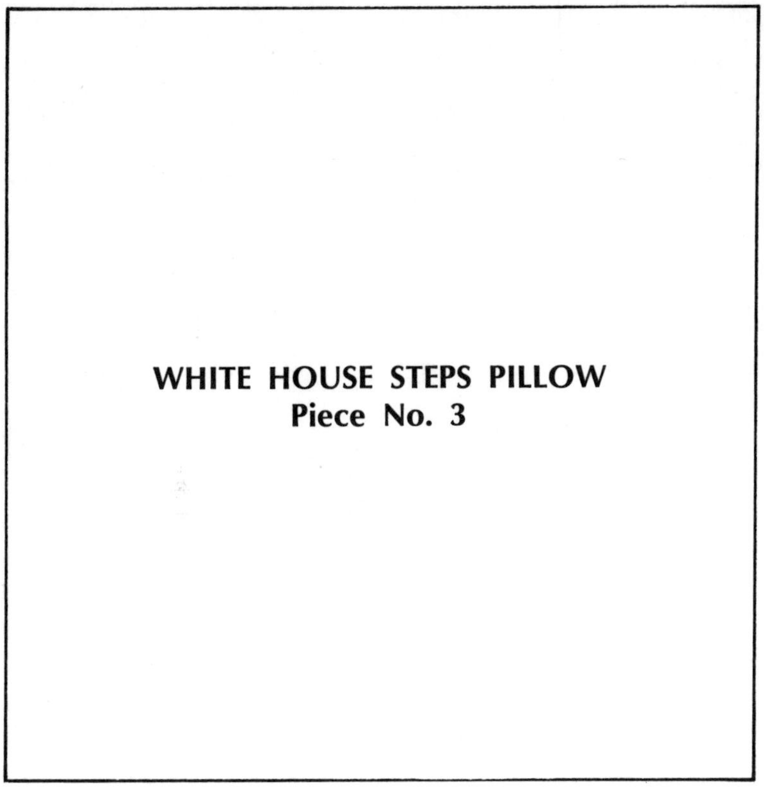
WHITE HOUSE STEPS PILLOW
Piece No. 3

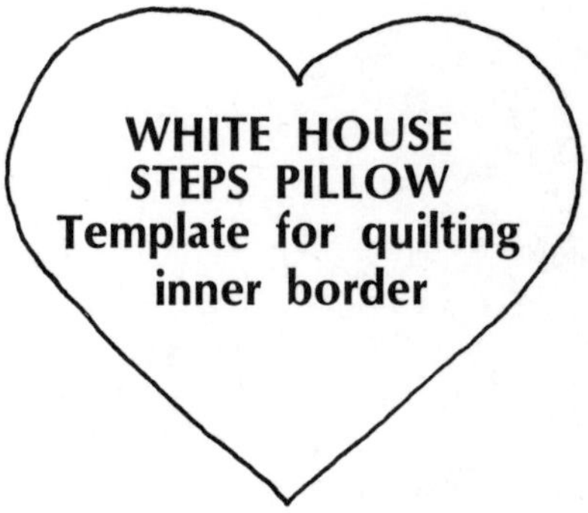
WHITE HOUSE
STEPS PILLOW
Template for quilting
inner border

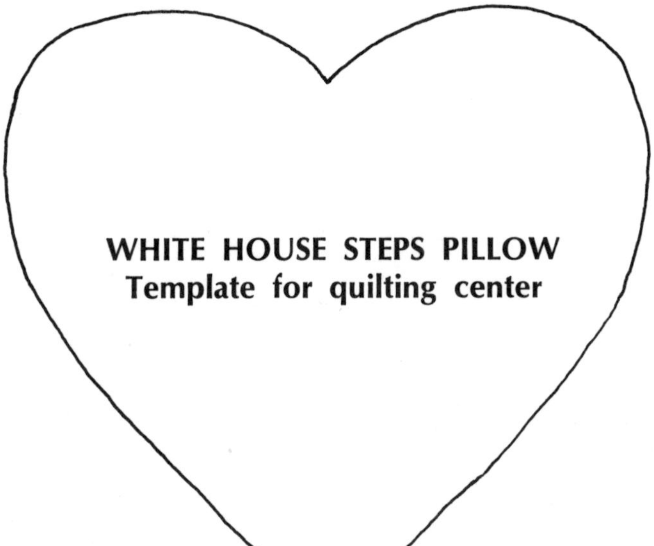
WHITE HOUSE STEPS PILLOW
Template for quilting center

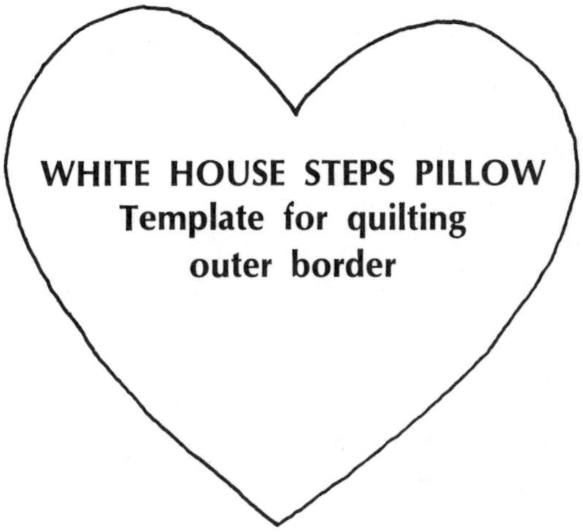
WHITE HOUSE STEPS PILLOW
Template for quilting
outer border

COMBINATION STAR PILLOW
Piece No. 2

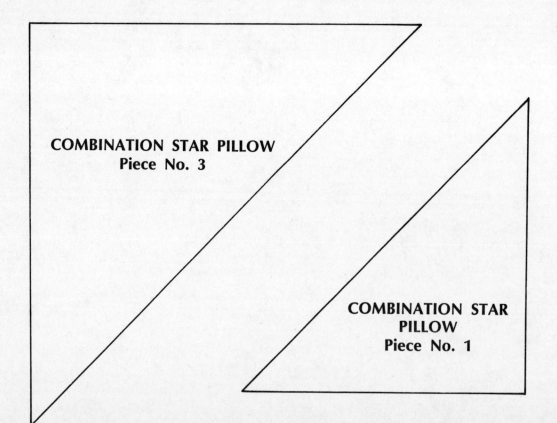

COMBINATION STAR PILLOW
Piece No. 3

COMBINATION STAR PILLOW
Piece No. 1

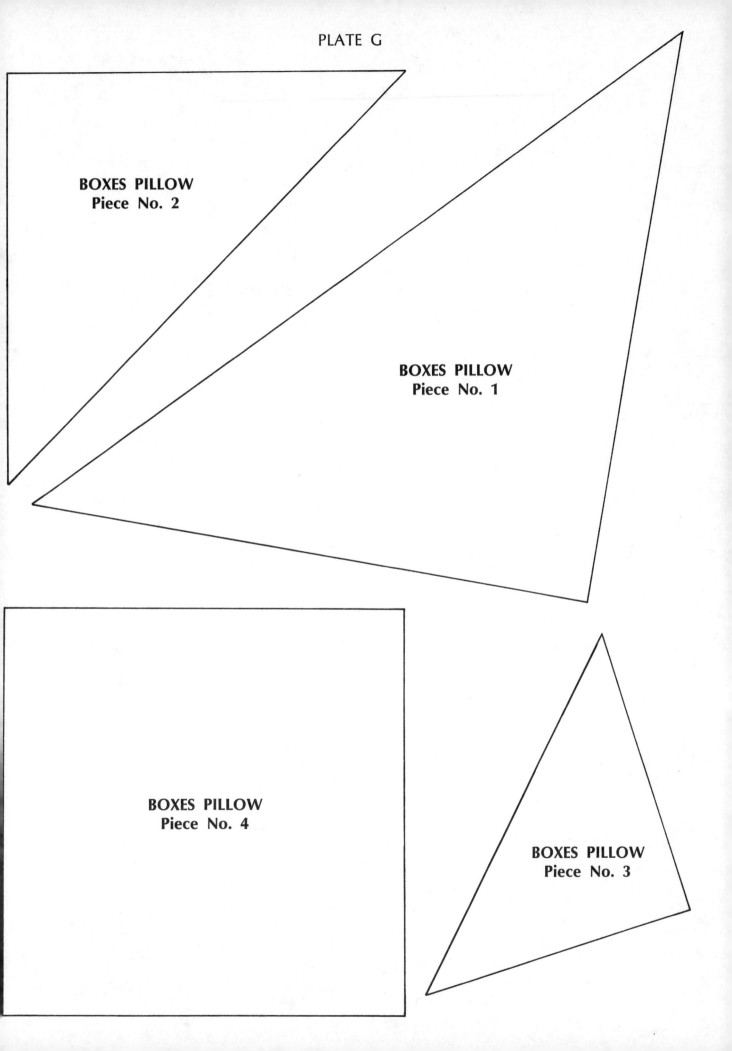

BOXES PILLOW
Piece No. 2

BOXES PILLOW
Piece No. 1

BOXES PILLOW
Piece No. 4

BOXES PILLOW
Piece No. 3

← PLACE ON FOLD OF FABRIC →

PINE TREE PILLOW
Piece No. 4

PINE TREE PILLOW
Piece No. 1

PLATE I

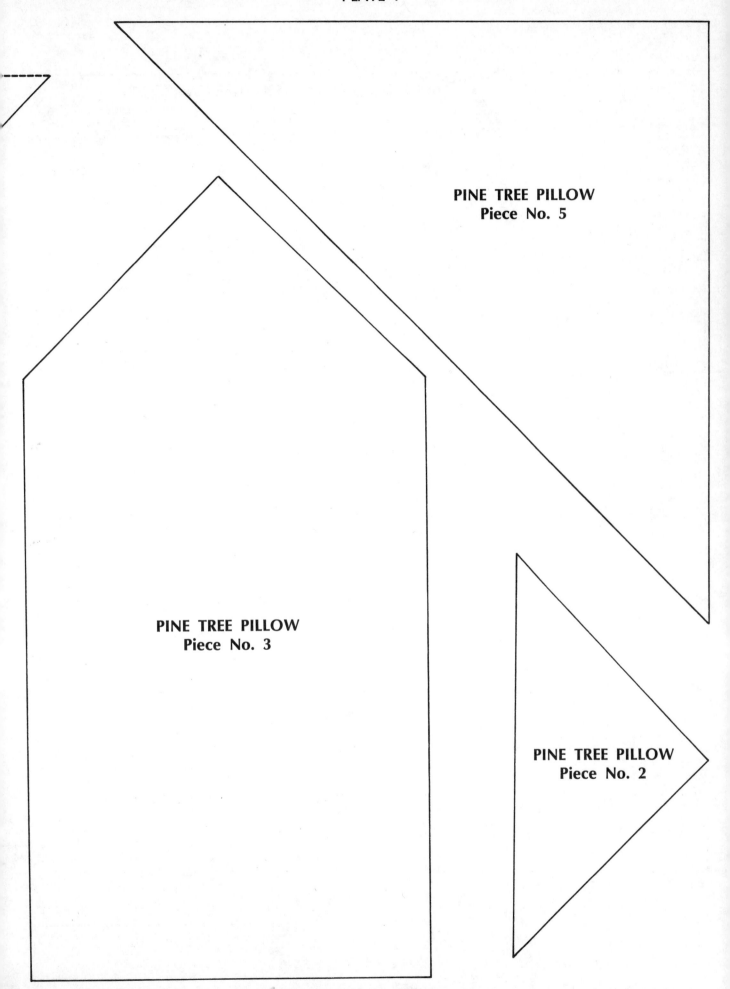

PINE TREE PILLOW
Piece No. 5

PINE TREE PILLOW
Piece No. 3

PINE TREE PILLOW
Piece No. 2

SPIDER'S WEB PILLOW
Piece No. 1

SPIDER'S WEB PILLOW
Piece No. 2

SPIDER'S WEB PILLOW
Piece No. 4

SPIDER'S WEB PILLOW
Piece No. 5

SPIDER'S WEB PILLOW
Piece No. 3

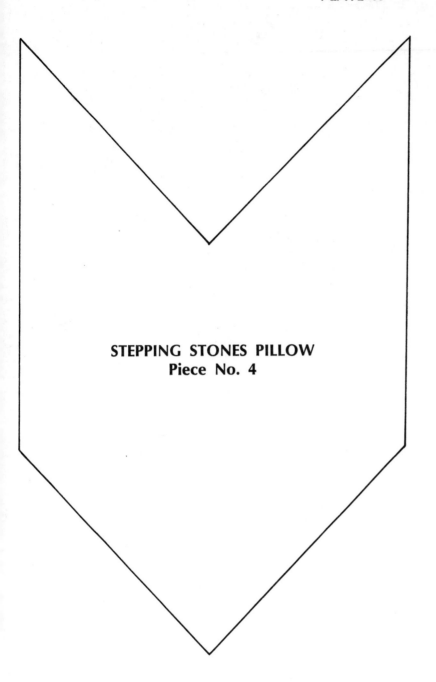

STEPPING STONES PILLOW
Piece No. 4

STEPPING STONES
PILLOW
Piece No. 2

STEPPING STONES
PILLOW
Piece No. 1

STEPPING STONES PILLOW
Piece No. 3

PLATE L

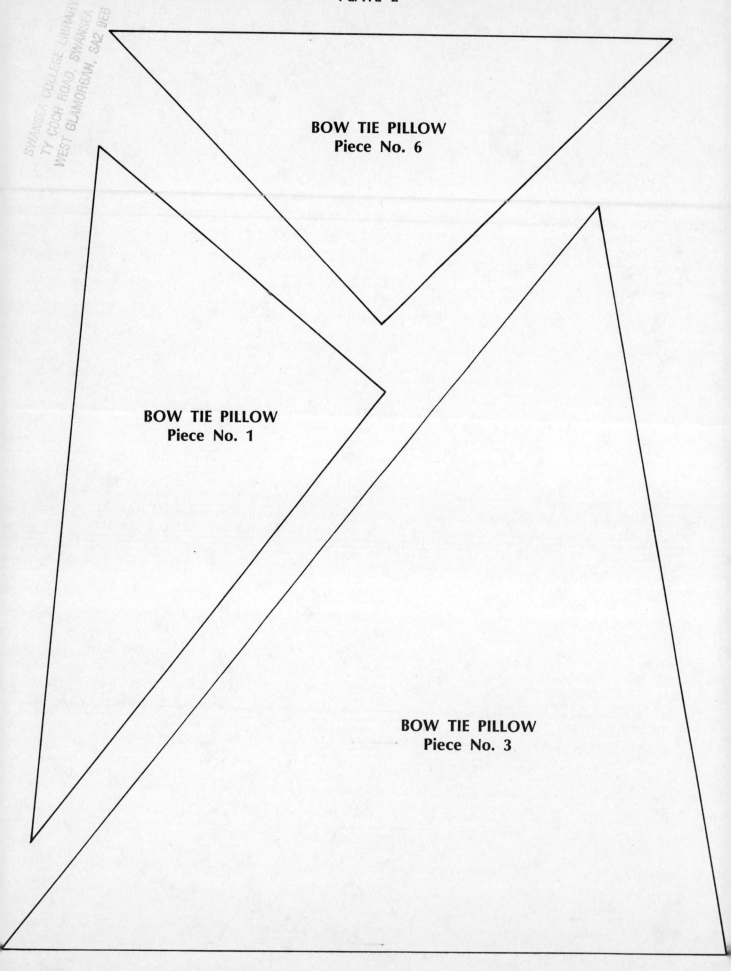

BOW TIE PILLOW
Piece No. 6

BOW TIE PILLOW
Piece No. 1

BOW TIE PILLOW
Piece No. 3

BOW TIE PILLOW
Piece No. 4

BOW TIE PILLOW
Piece No. 2

BOW TIE PILLOW
Piece No. 5

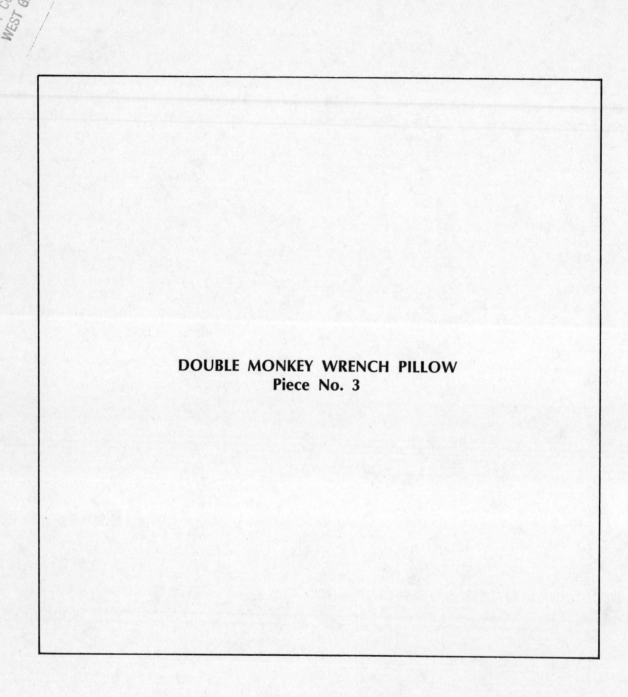

DOUBLE MONKEY WRENCH PILLOW
Piece No. 3

DOUBLE MONKEY WRENCH PILLOW
Piece No. 1

DOUBLE MONKEY WRENCH PILLOW
Piece No. 2

PLATE P

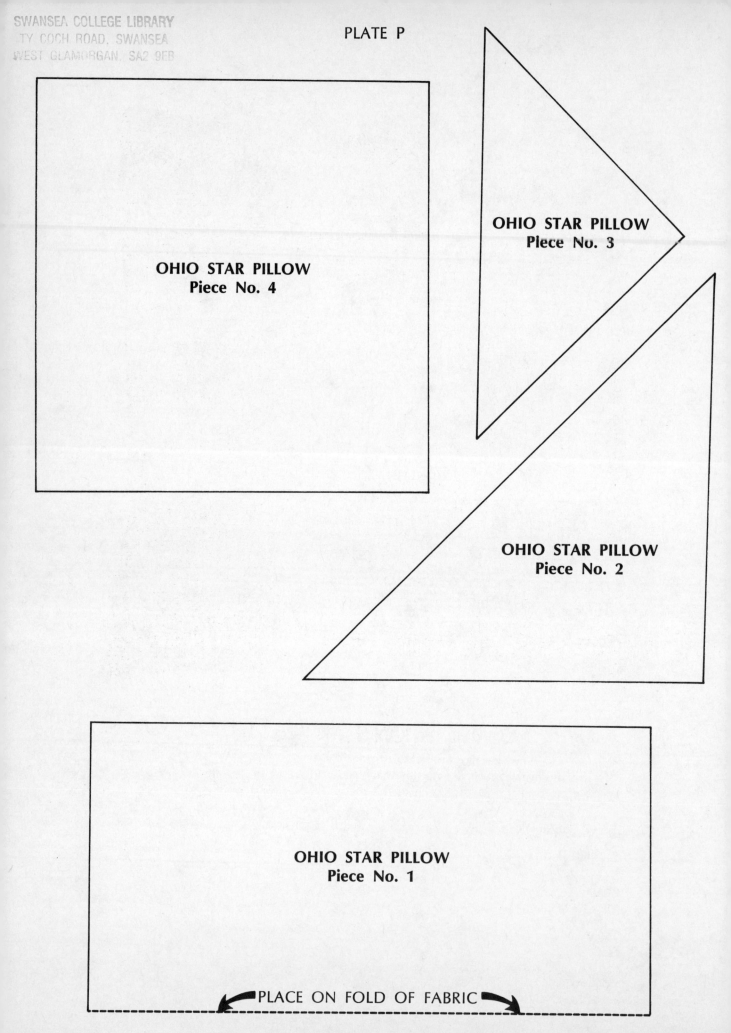

OHIO STAR PILLOW
Piece No. 4

OHIO STAR PILLOW
Piece No. 3

OHIO STAR PILLOW
Piece No. 2

OHIO STAR PILLOW
Piece No. 1

PLACE ON FOLD OF FABRIC

COMBINATION STAR PILLOW

This pillow was pieced partly by machine and partly by hand. The quilting was done by hand around each of the pieces made from template 2.

BOXES PILLOW

SIZE OF FINISHED PILLOW: 17" SQUARE

MATERIALS

¼ yard of each color fabric for piecing.
⅝ yard fabric for backing.

LEGEND

(BP) Blue Print
(RP) Red Print
(P) Red Plaid
(R) Red
(B) Blue
(WP) White Print

NUMBER OF PIECES TO BE CUT

Piece No. 1 ....4 White Print
Piece No. 1 ....4 Red Print
Piece No. 2 ....4 Red
Piece No. 2 ....8 Blue
Piece No. 2 ....4 Red Plaid
Piece No. 3 ....4 Blue Print
Piece No. 4 ....1 Red Plaid

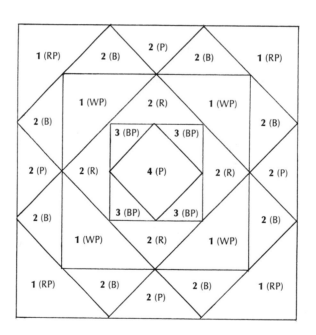

Templates for this pillow appear on Plate G.

12

BOXES PILLOW

This pillow was pieced and quilted by machine.

PINE TREE PILLOW

SIZE OF FINISHED PILLOW: 17″ SQUARE

MATERIALS

¼ yard of each color fabric except the green and red print, of which you will need 1/3 yard.

⅝ yard fabric for backing.

LEGEND

(GP) Green and Red Print
(RP) Red Print
(WP) Green and White Print
(P) Pink

NUMBER OF PIECES TO BE CUT

Piece No. 1 ....2 Red Print
Piece No. 2 ....18 Green and Red Print
Piece No. 2 ....18 Pink
Piece No. 3 ...1 Green and White Print
Piece No. 4 .....1 Green and Red Print
Piece No. 5 ....2 Red Print

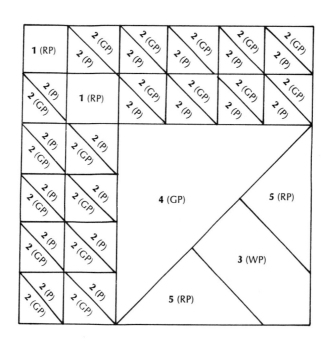

Templates for this pillow appear on Plates H and I.

14

PINE TREE PILLOW

This pillow was pieced by machine. The pillow is not quilted in the usual way but *tied* in the corners with embroidery floss. Do not knot the thread. Put the thread through the fabric from the right side, leaving about 1″ of thread on the right side. Bring the needle back up from the wrong to the right side; tie the thread in a knot, leaving ends about ½″ long; cut both threads to the same length. Repeat this procedure wherever you want to hold the fabric. The tied thread can form a pattern or be placed at random, as you wish.

SPIDER'S WEB PILLOW

SIZE OF FINISHED PILLOW: 15″ SQUARE

MATERIALS

¼ yard of each color fabric for piecing.
½ yard fabric for backing.

LEGEND

(B) Blue
(BS) Blue Stripes
(BG) Blue Gingham
(S) Brown Stripes
(Y) Yellow

NUMBER OF PIECES TO BE CUT

Piece No. 1 ....4 Blue
Piece No. 2 ....4 Blue Gingham
Piece No. 3 ....4 Blue Stripes
Piece No. 4 ....4 Yellow
Piece No. 5 ....4 Brown Stripes

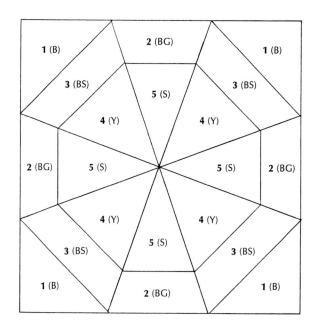

Templates for this pillow appear on Plate J.

SPIDER'S WEB PILLOW

This pillow was pieced and quilted by hand.

STEPPING STONES PILLOW

SIZE OF FINISHED PILLOW: 15″ SQUARE

MATERIALS

¼ yard of each color fabric for piecing.
½ yard fabric for backing.

LEGEND

(R) Red
(RP) Red Print
(B) Black Print
(Y) Yellow
(G) Green
(P) Pink

NUMBER OF PIECES TO BE CUT

Piece No. 1 . . . . .24 Pink
Piece No. 1 . . . . .2 Red
Piece No. 1 . . . . .2 Yellow
Piece No. 1 . . . . .12 Black Print
Piece No. 2 . . . . .4 Green
Piece No. 3 . . . . .8 Green
Piece No. 4 . . . . .4 Red Print

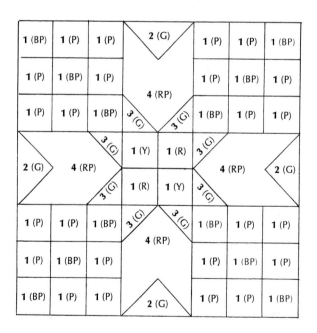

Templates for this pillow appear on Plate K.

18

STEPPING STONES PILLOW

This pillow was pieced by machine and quilted by machine around the pieces made by template 4. It is tied in the center with embroidery floss. Do not knot the thread. Put the thread through the fabric from the right side, leaving about 1″ of thread on the right side. Bring the needle back up from the wrong to the right side; tie the thread in a knot, leaving ends about ½″ long; cut both threads to the same length. Join the small squares made from template 1 together before joining them to the other pieces.

BOW TIE PILLOW

SIZE OF FINISHED PILLOW: 17″ SQUARE WITHOUT RUFFLE

MATERIALS

¼ yard of each color fabric for piecing.
⅝ yard fabric for backing.
See introduction for fabric requirements
    for ruffling.

LEGEND

(P) Pink
(PG) Pink Gingham
(Y) Yellow
(G) Green
(GP) Green Print
(YP) Yellow Print

NUMBER OF PIECES TO BE CUT

Piece No. 1 ....4 Pink
Piece No. 2 ....2 Yellow Print
Piece No. 2, *reversed*....2 Yellow Print
Piece No. 3 ....2 Yellow
Piece No. 4 ....2 Pink Gingham
Piece No. 5 ....2 Green
Piece No. 5, *reversed* ....2 Green
Piece No. 6 ....2 Pink
Piece No. 6 ....2 Green Print

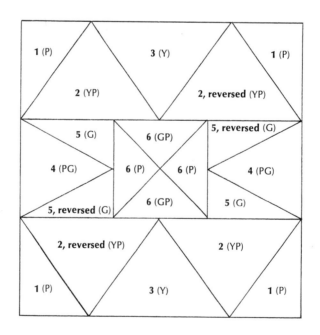

Templates for this pillow appear on Plates L and M.

BOW TIE PILLOW

This pillow was pieced by machine and quilted by hand. See page vi for instructions on adding the ruffle.

DOUBLE MONKEY WRENCH PILLOW

SIZE OF FINISHED PILLOW: 17″ SQUARE

MATERIALS

¼ yard of each color fabric for piecing.
⅝ yard fabric for backing.

LEGEND

(G) Green
(L) Lavender
(P) Purple
(O) Orange
(PR) Print

NUMBER OF PIECES TO BE CUT

Piece No. 1 . . . . .4 Green
Piece No. 1 . . . . .4 Lavender
Piece No. 2 . . . . .4 Purple
Piece No. 2 . . . . .4 Orange
Piece No. 3 . . . . .1 Print

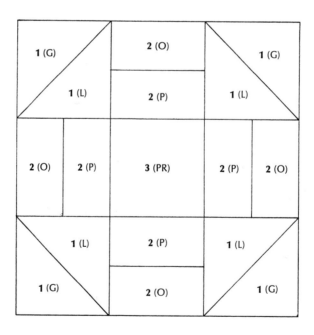

Templates for this pillow appear on Plates N and O.

DOUBLE MONKEY WRENCH PILLOW

This pillow was pieced and quilted by machine.

OHIO STAR PILLOW

SIZE OF FINISHED PILLOW: 17″ SQUARE WITHOUT RIBBON BORDER

MATERIALS

¼ yard of each color fabric for piecing.
⅝ yard fabric for backing without ribbon border. If ribbon is added, 2/3 yard of backing material will be needed.
Ribbon border requires 2 yards of each ribbon.

LEGEND

(BP) Black Print
(B) Black
(R) Red
(RP) Red Print
(G) Green

NUMBER OF PIECES TO BE CUT

Piece No. 1 . . . . 4 Black Print
Piece No. 2. . . . . .8 Red
Piece No. 2 . . . . .8 Black
Piece No. 3. . . . . .4 Green
Piece No. 4 . . . . .1 Red Print

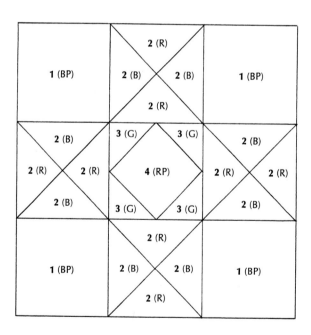

Templates for this pillow appear on Plate P.

24

OHIO STAR PILLOW

This pillow was pieced by machine and quilted by hand. The ribbon border, made up of two different grosgrain ribbons—one 1″ wide and the other ¼″—was machine-stitched on after the quilting was completed. The backing fabric was then sewn to the ribbon.

DOVER BOOKS ON QUILTING, CROCHET, KNITTING AND OTHER AREAS

Paperbound unless otherwise indicated. Prices subject to change without notice. Available at your book dealer or write for free catalogues to Dept. Needlework, Dover Publications, Inc., 180 Varick Street, New York, N.Y. 10014. Please indicate field of interest. Each year Dover publishes over 200 books on fine art, music, crafts and needlework, antiques, languages, literature, children's books, chess, cookery, nature, anthropology, science, mathematics, and other areas.

Manufactured in the U.S.A.